Traditions Around The

Jewellery and Accessories

11.2

by Louise Tythacott

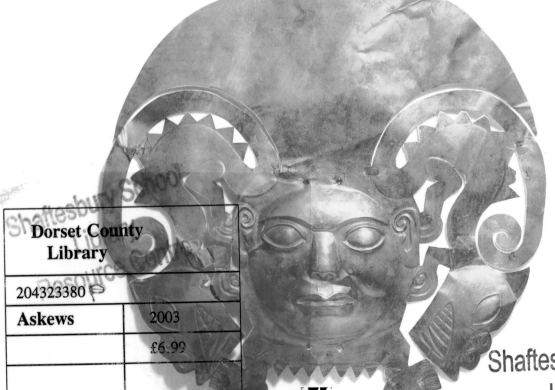

W
HODDER
Wayland

Traditions Around The World

Other titles in the Traditions Around The World series:

Body Decoration

Costumes

Jewellery and Accessories

Masks

Musical Instruments

Editor: Katie Roden
Designer: Loraine Hayes
Cover design: Hodder Wayland
Consultant: Anthony Shelton, Keeper of Non-Western Art and Anthropology, Royal Pavilion Art Gallery and Museums, Brighton, East Sussex, England.

First published in 1994 by Wayland (Publishers) Ltd
This paperback edition revised and updated in 2003

© Hodder Wayland 1994

British Library Cataloguing in Publication Data

Tythacott, Louise
  Jewellery and Accessories. – (Traditions Around The World Series)
  I. Title II. Series
  391.7

ISBN 0 7502 4526 3

Typeset by Avon DataSet Ltd, Bidford on Avon
Printed and bound in Italy by G. Canale and C.S.p.A.

COVER: A Burmese woman wearing traditional jewellery around her neck.

Picture acknowledgements:

The publishers wish to thank the following for providing the photographs for this book: British Museum 6, 7, 9, 10–11; Chapel Studios 28 (Zul Mukhida); Corbis *cover* (Kevin R. Morris); Sue Cunningham 22, 24, 25, 38; Robert Harding Picture library 4–5 (top), 12, 18, 26, 44; Life File 11 (0. Svyatolavsky); Tony Stone Worldwide 2 (both, left N. DeVore), 4–5 (bottom, D. Torckler), 27 (N. DeVore), 30 (H. Kavanagh), 32, 37, 42 (D. Torckler); Wayland Picture Library 5(top right), 33; Werner Forman Archive 1 (Museum of the American Indian, USA), 4 (bottom left), 14–15 (Plains Indians Museum, USA), 15 (Alaska Gallery of Eskimo Art), 21 (Museum of the American Indian), 23, 29 (Schindler Collection, New York), 34–5, 36, 40–41, 43 (Museum of Mankind, UK); Zefa Picture Library 16–17.

The artwork is by Peter Bull.

Contents

Jewellery and accessories around the world

The foot of Nana Owusu Sampa III, an Asante king from Ghana. ▼

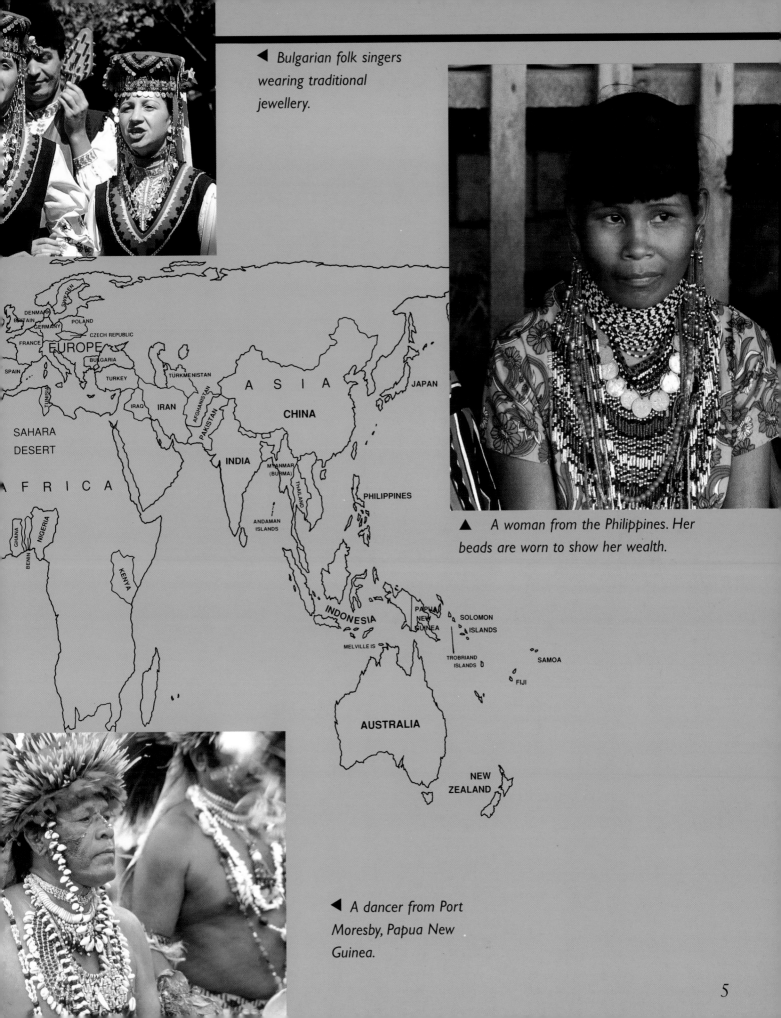

◄ Bulgarian folk singers wearing traditional jewellery.

▲ A woman from the Philippines. Her beads are worn to show her wealth.

◄ A dancer from Port Moresby, Papua New Guinea.

5

Introduction

Jewellery is one of the oldest forms of decorative art. A necklace has been discovered in Arpachiya (modern Iraq) that was made over 7,000 years ago, and a pendant has been found in Africa which is believed to be about 15,000 years old. Jewellery is also one of the most modern and inventive art forms. Nowadays, amongst the Wahgi people in Papua New Guinea, bubble-gum wrappers, bottle tops and sardine cans are used to adorn the body.

Jewellery is made and worn for many purposes – to show power, wealth and status, for protection and healing, to show strength and courage, to send messages, or simply to make the wearer look more beautiful. Among certain peoples in Africa, women are only considered beautiful when they wear thousands of colourful glass beads around their necks. On the other hand, other peoples in Africa are known to 'decorate' their women to make them look uglier, so that they will not be stolen by other peoples and used as slaves.

Jewellery can be created from many things. In cultures where gold, silver and precious stones are rare and expensive, jewellery made from these materials shows importance or wealth. However, in other cultures different materials are valued, and jewellery can be made from shells, bones, teeth, feathers or hair, and even newspaper, plastic or old tin.

Around the world, jewellery is worn by both men and women. In Europe and North America, women wear more decoration than men, but in other parts of the world it is often the men who are the most colourful and ornate.

Jewellery can be either functional – such as a brooch or pin to fasten clothing – or seen as an art form. Modern artists create 'designer' jewellery, and some Native American groups sell their bracelets and necklaces in art galleries.

However it has been made, and whatever it has been made for, jewellery has played an important part in the lives of men and women for centuries, and will surely continue to do so for centuries to come.

◀ (Main picture) This court jewellery is from Ur, Sumeria, and is about 4,500 years old.

◀ (Far left) The ancient Egyptians wore much jewellery. This detail of a wall painting shows female musicians wearing gold earrings, bangles and amulets. It is from the tomb of Nebamun at Thebes, built about 3,500 years ago.

7

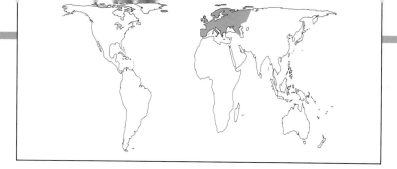

Europe

Today in Europe, many people wear jewellery as a form of decoration. Anyone can wear jewels, from children to old people, but men tend to wear less decoration than women. Nowadays it is possible to buy many different types of jewellery, from cheap plastic trinkets to the expensive gold and silver jewels sold in exclusive shops. Decoration can be worn all over the body, but people generally wear ornaments on their ears and fingers, and around their necks and wrists.

Jewellery is even seen as an art form: famous designers, such as Fabergé, have created pieces that are considered to be modern art. The Surrealist painter Salvador Dali, for example, designed earrings in the shape of telephone receivers, and rings that looked like snails. Modern designers use a variety of materials to create their jewellery. Some use discarded lampshades or perspex, and some even paint chicken and animal bones with enamel.

People have been wearing jewellery in Europe for thousands of years. Hoards of Bronze and Iron Age brooches, pins and arm rings have been found, mostly in burial sites. The Celts made many different types of jewellery, but the most common ornament was the brooch. This was worn on one or both shoulders, and was used to fasten cloaks.

These early pieces probably had magical functions, too – they may have served as amulets to protect the wearer from harm. The Celts also put jewellery on the bodies of the dead, so that most of the ancient pieces now in museums have come from graves. The Anglo-Saxons and

▲ A dragon-shaped brooch from early Britain. This dates from the second century AD, and is made of bronze and enamel.

Vikings made many brooches, pins and necklaces from silver and gold, and buried them with the dead.

By the mid-sixteenth century, Spain was the richest country in Europe, because of all the gold and precious stones which arrived there from Central and South America. The leading goldsmiths and jewellers of the time moved from court to court, from the kingdoms of northern Europe and Britain down to Italy and Spain. At this time, jewels were worn as much by men as by women, to show their status in society.

The kings and queens of Europe had the finest jewels of all. Today, royal families in Britain, Sweden and Denmark all have wonderful crown jewels that have been collected over hundreds of years. Some are still worn for public ceremonies such as coronations. These collections are usually open to the public, but are always under tight security – for obvious reasons!

Crowns and jewels are also worn by villagers and townspeople in Europe, but these are made from much less valuable materials. A brightly decorated bridal crown was traditionally the most important feature of a woman's wedding outfit. Nowadays in Denmark, the head-dress of the bride has gold and silver thread embroidery, pearls, silk ribbons and small pieces of mirror. In Germany, bridal gowns are adorned with pieces of material, paper and gold leaf, to which flowers, glass, fruit, sheet metal, gold sequins and glass spheres are sometimes attached.

Rings are a very popular form of jewellery in Europe, and they have been used for centuries, for many different purposes. From the fourteenth century onwards, it was popular to wear a ring in memory of a dead relative or friend, and some rings contained the hair of a loved one. Rings could also be worn as a symbol of wealth, and at funerals in Victorian Britain different types of gift ring would be given to the mourners according to their status.

Nowadays in Europe, rings are frequently given for engagements and marriages. In France, for example, 'rings of faith or promise' are still given to seal the engagement between young people before their official engagement.

Gold rings from the Thetford ▶
treasure, found in Norfolk,
England, in 1976. They were
made in the fourth century AD.

▲ *The bride and groom both wear crowns in this traditional church wedding in Rostov, southern Russia.*

Rings and other jewellery were traditionally presented as a token of love. In the Czech Republic this could be in the form of a comb, necklace, ring or brooch. In Poland, boys used to offer beads and brooches to their sweethearts. These tokens were often made in a form which suggested love and marriage – necklaces or rings were made in the shape of hearts, clasped hands, padlocks, or Adam and Eve. You could also find the name or initials of the person, and sometimes a longer inscription.

Elaborate jewellery is still worn on special occasions in the countryside in Bulgaria. Young married women wear an ornament called a prochelnik on their forehead or hat. Pendants known as kabuti are attached to the headscarf, and a chain of coins called a podbradnik is worn under the chin to hold a hat in place. All the best clothes and heavy silver jewellery are worn on special festivals such as Lazarouvane, the festival of youth, which takes place eight days before Easter.

These Bulgarian folk singers in national costume ▶ wear a chain called a prochelnik on their foreheads, a podbradnik chain under their chins and an ornate gold buckle around their waists.

Jewellery is also worn in Bulgaria for protection. A married woman traditionally wears a large, ornate, silver buckle around her waist to protect her abdomen when she is at work in the fields. Jewellery is also associated with magic. On the first Sunday before Lent, the peasants hold a festival which marks the beginning of spring. Here, men dress in masks and wear large, heavy, silver bells around their waists. The noise of these bells is believed to drive away evil and sickness. On St George's Day, a bride is supposed to milk the first ewe through a ring to ensure a plentiful supply of milk for the summer. In the past, a ring was buried with the dead, as it was believed to help them on their journey to the other world. This ring could also be used to treat illness: if, for example, you had a nosebleed, you could stop it by placing the ring under your nose so that the drops of blood passed through it. In times of epidemics, Bulgarian women used to wear all their metal jewellery, and put a gold or silver coin in their mouth.

Although some of this jewellery still exists today, the traditions are not as strong as they were in the past. Nowadays it is only the old women who have the jewellery, which they have kept from their youth.

The jewellery sold in modern Turkey is often brilliantly coloured. Gold and silver are popular, but other materials are also used. Many blue glass talismans are made and sold, both to tourists and to Turkish people, in jewellery shops and bazaars. Some of these talismans are round or oval pendants made of thick, bright blue glass, with an eye painted in the centre. These are believed to protect against the evil eye. In Turkey, Bulgaria, India and other countries around the world, people believe that an angry look or glance can cause harm or injury, especially to children. To protect themselves from such a look – the evil eye – people may attach amulets or charms to the clothes of babies and young children.

Make a jewelled crown

You will need:
thick paper, 70 cm long, 22 cm wide
pencil
scissors
glue
ruler
milk bottle tops
glitter
silver tinsel
red ribbons

1. Fold the paper lengthways into two, open it up, and draw a line along the centre crease. Using the ruler, measure and draw six triangles along the top half, and cut them out.

2. Wrap the paper around your head so that the triangles point upwards. Check that it fits, by making sure that the ends of the paper meet.

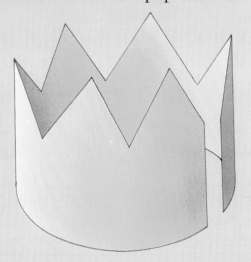

3. Glue the glitter, tinsel and bottle tops on to the paper. Glue the two ends together to create a crown, and stick on the red ribbons so that they hang down at the sides.

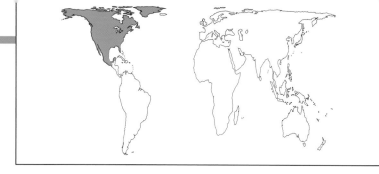

North America

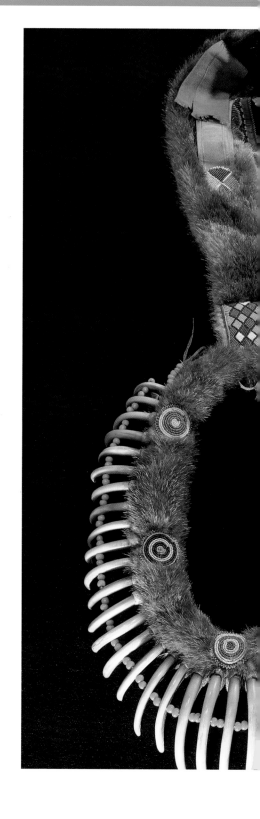

Today in North America, many people wear jewellery in a similar way to Europeans. Fashionable jewellers in big cities like New York, San Francisco and Toronto sell modern designs using expensive materials, such as gold and precious stones.

But long before Europeans arrived in the USA in the sixteenth and seventeenth centuries, the Native Americans had their own culture and traditions. In the 2,000-year-old burial sites of the Hopewell people, jewellery made of pearls, copper, silver and shells has been found.

When the Europeans arrived, some of the Native Americans were killed and others were forced to migrate. Much of the traditional culture from this period was lost or destroyed. Fortunately, some of the jewellery and decorative art forms of the past are being produced again today.

Originally, beadwork was an important form of decoration. Beads were made of local materials such as shells, grass, seeds, silver berries or dried rosehips. Such materials were made into earrings, necklaces and armbands. Shell beads were known as wampum and were attached to belts and costumes. Wampum was traded as money and used in special ceremonies. In some areas, beaded belts were used to send messages to other groups. Sending a white belt meant peace, but if a purple belt was sent it could mean a declaration of war. Beads were so important in Native American culture that when the Europeans first arrived they offered glass beads to the Native Americans, to establish friendship.

▲ This bear-claw necklace was made by the Fox people, who lived on the fringes of the Plains and Great Lakes cultures. It was worn as a mark of status to show great bravery.

14

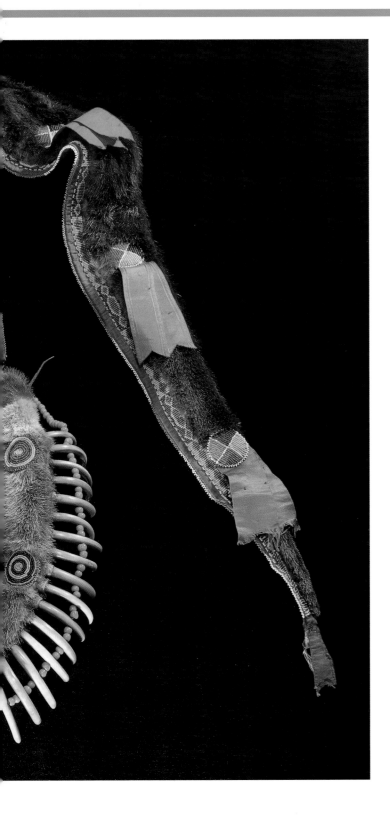

Eventually these European glass beads became more popular than shell beads, and gave the Native American jewellery a more colourful appearance.

Jewellery was used to indicate wealth, status and bravery. The Blackfoot people of the northern Plains made necklaces from bear claws. These were very valuable because they indicated that the wearer was a brave hunter. Natural yellow claws were the most important and were often worn by the Blackfoot, Crow and Western Sioux peoples. During the second half of the nineteenth century, the grizzly bear population declined because there was too much hunting, so imitation claws were carved from cow horns, hooves and wood. Today, bear-claw necklaces are still popular, but are made of synthetic materials such as plastic.

This small ivory carving of a human is decorated with blue beads and was made by the Inuit in Alaska. It was probably used as a charm and was hung around the wearer's neck. ▶

Jewellery was traditionally worn to indicate bravery and status amongst Native American peoples. This group of modern-day Shoshone men are wearing feather head-dresses and bead jewellery in a similar way to their ancestors. ▶

The Sioux in the Plains also valued bravery, and this was reflected in their jewellery. Feathers were worn in the hair to show an individual's courage. A red dot painted on a feather indicated the way in which an enemy had been killed. Tufts of hair taken from the heads of enemies were attached to the arms and legs. The most stunning ornaments of all were the long feather head-dresses, which sometimes reached down to the ground. They were usually made from eagle and owl feathers, and were worn on ceremonial occasions. The eagle was considered a sacred animal to the Plains peoples, and its feathers were prized for medicine as well as ornamentation.

Along the north-west Pacific coast of America, jewellery is still being made and worn by some of the Native American peoples. These peoples live near the ocean and the forest, and many of the elements in their art and mythology are taken from the local environment. The raven, eagle, killer whale, shark, frog and hawk are popular, and many clans are named after these animals. Silver and gold bracelets, necklaces, brooches and rings are engraved with animal faces and used today by families as their crests. The raven is one of the most important figures in the mythology of the Haida people, whose silver bracelets often show a raven's eyes and beak. The bracelets were originally made from beaten silver coins and were worn by women as decoration. Today, these bracelets and jewellery are made by silversmiths who may sell them commercially to tourists.

In the frozen lands of northern Canada and Alaska, the Inuit people create their decorative jewellery from walrus ivory and glass beads. Both men and women wear long glass-bead

earrings, and lip plugs made of ivory and stone. Traditionally, the women used to wear delicate ivory plugs, whereas the men wore larger plugs as they got older. Because it was uncomfortable to wear lip plugs when it was very cold, the Inuit took them out when they travelled. They would replace them when they arrived at the next village, so that they were properly adorned. In western Alaska, headbands made from strips of fur and sheep's teeth were worn for whaling. At the centre of these headbands hung a stone in the shape of a whale – a kind of good luck charm. Most Inuit jewellery is small and compact so that it can be carried easily from camp to camp. Small, functional objects are also made from ivory, such as button fastenings, combs and snow goggles.

In the south-west of North America, near the Mexican border, live the Navajo people. They are the largest surviving Native American group in North America. The Navajo have kept their colourful dances and ceremonies alive, and have retained their traditional skills as silversmiths. They have worn fine silver jewellery since the sixteenth century, when they learnt the art of silversmithing from the Mexican peoples. In the nineteenth century they supplied European traders with rings, bracelets, earrings and necklaces made from silver, with turquoise and other precious stones inlaid.

During the early twentieth century, traders encouraged Native American peoples to produce jewellery specifically for the tourist market. Nowadays, Native American craft guilds have been set up to help maintain high standards, and Navajo silver jewellery can be found in art galleries all over the world.

For the Aztec and Maya in Mexico, turquoise and jade were more precious than gold. The Aztec believed that because turquoise was blue, it was like the sky and the water. Amongst the Maya, small balls of jade were placed in the mouths of the dead to indicate that they would live forever after death.

The Navajo people in the south-west of the USA have kept their jewellery traditions alive. They are well known for their skills at making turquoise and silver bracelets, necklaces and rings. ▶

The Huichol people live on top of the canyons in north-west Mexico. The women make bead bracelets, necklaces, pendants and rings with very complex patterns for both men and women. The Huichol say that the patterns are given to them by their gods. Some look like the markings on a snake, and others represent sacred plants and flowers. For the Huichol, the quality of the beadwork on a piece of jewellery indicates a woman's devotion to the gods.

Decorate your hair with feathers

You will need:
3 feathers
red paint
paintbrush

1. Paint a red dot on each feather.

2. Stick the feathers in your hair to indicate bravery, like the Sioux people of the North American Plains.

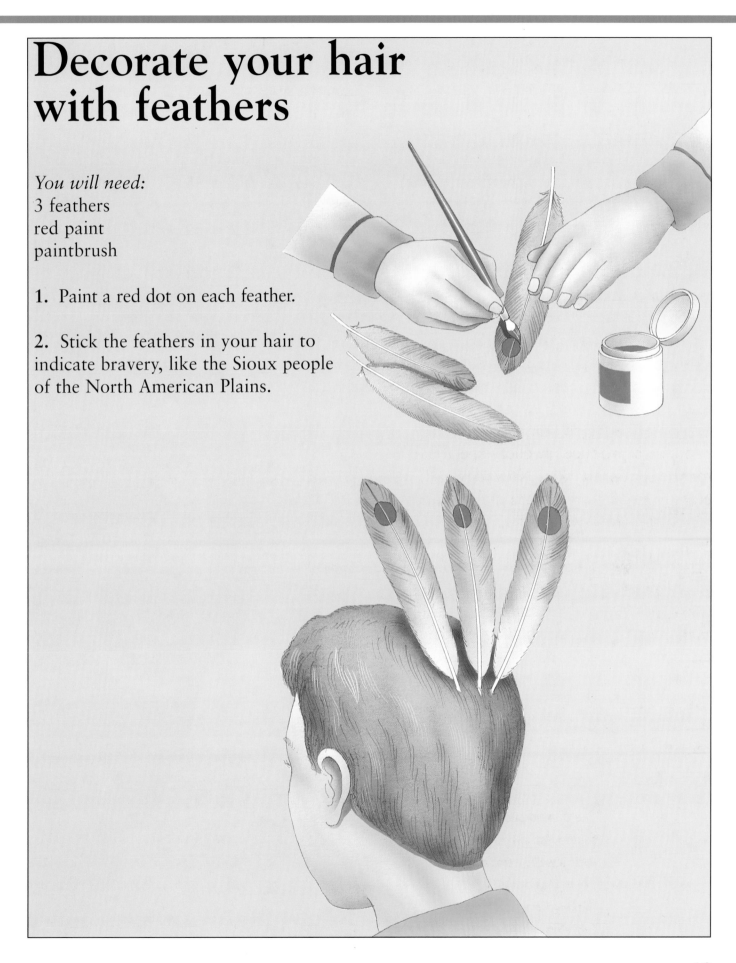

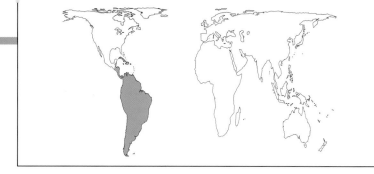

Central and South America

Jewellery has an ancient history in Central and South America. Long before the Spanish arrived in the sixteenth century, the Maya and Inca peoples had civilizations in which dress, body decoration and art were very highly developed.

Stone carvings made by the Maya people in Central America show that the high-ranking nobles wore a great variety of costumes and ornaments. Jade was the favourite material, used to make nose pins, ear plugs and necklaces. Jade jewellery was often buried with the dead, and the number of jade pieces in a person's tomb was an indication of his or her wealth and importance.

Gold was an important material to the peoples of ancient Central and South America. This gold mask pendant is from the Chimu culture of Peru in the thirteenth century AD. On either side of the face are two dragon-like animals, which were associated with status. ▶

In ancient South America, gold was called 'the Sweat of the Sun', whilst silver was 'the Tears of the Moon'. Gold was the most important material to the Inca people in Peru, who associated it with their sun god, Inti. Only the ruler of the Incas was allowed to wear jewellery made of this material.

Early South American jewellery was often very colourful and made from many materials, including bright tropical birds' feathers, human hair, animal teeth, delicate fish bones and beetle wings.

In Colombia, jewellery and precious objects have been found at the bottom of sacred lakes. At lake Guatavita, a special ceremony used to be performed to welcome each new ruler. The old ruler was covered in gold dust and would go out on a raft and throw piles of jewellery into the lake. Sometimes he would dive into the water. The old ruler was known as El Dorado – 'The Gilded Man'.

When the Spanish conquered South America in the sixteenth century, the beautiful gold and jade jewellery was plundered, and sometimes re-cast into European-style jewellery. Today, the peoples of South and Central America have lost many of their ancient traditions, but much of their jewellery is still made from feathers, skins, bones, minerals and traded beads.

Feathers are especially important to the peoples in the Amazon rain forests in South America. They are used in head-dresses to indicate the age, status and identity of the wearer. Amongst the Cashinahua of eastern Peru, the most spectacular head-dresses are worn for the headman's dance, which is frequently associated with fertility. Bright red macaw tail-feathers, white feathers from the breast of the harpy eagle, and black turkey feathers are used. There is also a 'spirit' head-dress, worn by dancers who are imitating the spirits.

▲ *A South American feather head-dress, from the Amazon basin.*

23

▲ *A Yanomani man carrying feathers that he has just collected, to be made into jewellery.*

Monkey-teeth collars are always made and worn by men. Children wear necklaces made from the teeth and bones of dangerous animals, such as the sting rae, to protect themselves from attack. Other necklaces are made from animals that are admired by the Cashinahua. The ocelot is a sly and stealthy animal, and young men wear ocelot-teeth jewellery in the hope that they, too, may become cunning and successful hunters.

In other places in Central and South America, metal ornaments are popular, and silver is often used. The Araucanian people of Chile have a long history of metalworking. Large, circular pendants are worn by the headmen of a clan, and pendants, bracelets, anklets and rings are worn by both men and women. In the Andes, a popular ornament is a metal pin known as a tapu. Tapus are elaborately decorated, and women use them to fasten their cloaks. Amongst the Mapuche of Chile, women often wear a chain with coins and pendants attached around the forehead and across the breast. However, when the Chilean cowboys use these chains, they put them on their horses and use them as reins.

The Cashinahua wear collars round their necks made from seeds and monkey teeth. The most valuable collar is made of eight strands of monkey teeth – about 850 individual teeth. Monkeys are a very important source of food in the rain forest, and a man who has enough monkey teeth to make a collar of this size shows that he is a very good hunter.

Feathers and beads are worn as decoration amongst the Kayapo in Brazil. Feathers are taken from the local environment but beads, such as these blue, red and white ones, are imported. ▶

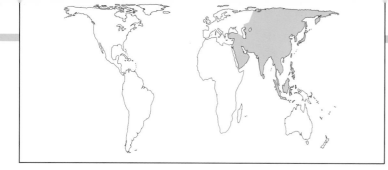

Asia

The jewellery worn in Asia is very varied and has been made for many thousands of years. Finely polished pendants and beads which are over 5,000 years old have been found in China. Jade is considered more valuable than gold or silver in China because it has always been associated with health, luck and beauty. In ancient China, only court officials could wear belt hooks made of jade, and the tinkling of a jade ornament hanging from a belt was the sign of a gentleman.

Traditionally in China, brides used to wear stunningly beautiful head-dresses made of silver and gold. These were adorned with vivid blue kingfisher feathers, red flowers, butterflies, pearls, strands of red coral and white glass beads.

Japanese women often wear wooden combs and hairpins, and brides bring their own set of combs along with them on their wedding day. It is a wedding tradition for a woman to put a comb in her hair and only throw it away if she wants a divorce. There is an ancient belief that the soul of the wearer lives between the teeth of a comb, and in Japan people think it is bad luck to pick up a comb that has been thrown away or lost.

▲ A bride from the Miao people, in Taigong, China. She is wearing the traditional bridal jewellery of the Miao. Styles of head-dress are very different amongst the different peoples of China.

In Japan, combs and hairpins are used to show off a woman's hairstyle. In the past, women sometimes wore so many combs and pins that they had to sleep with their neck on a special pillow to keep everything in place. ▶

In Indonesia, jewellery is associated with magic and healing. This amulet from Borneo is used by a shaman to heal people. The shaman takes small chips of wood from the amulet and makes them into a cure. ▶

Jewellery is worn all over India for a variety of reasons, but it is often linked to marriage. Traditionally, women do not always meet their husbands before marriage. If a woman wants to see what her future husband looks like, she can wear a ring with a mirror on it. At the wedding ceremony she looks down into the mirror to see his face. The bride wears as much jewellery as her family can afford, and she may not take it off for months after the wedding, as this is considered bad luck. If her husband dies, she must smash all her ornaments and remove all her jewellery.

In southern India, the husband ties a special gold pendant around the neck of his wife during the marriage ceremony to announce their union. In northern India, rural married women wear ornaments on their forehead or nose. Some of their nose rings are so large and elaborate that they hang down over the mouth and must be lifted when the women eat.

Amongst Muslim and some Hindu groups, a woman who is married should not be seen in public by men who are not relatives. She wears a lot of bells on her jewellery to warn that she is approaching. The bells are also used to ward off scorpions, snakes and evil spirits.

Jewellery is sometimes worn as an amulet in India, to protect the wearer from harm. These amulets are often pendants made of silver, gold and precious stones, but plants, animals and cowrie shells can also be used. Some amulets are used to protect children. Jhoria-Muria boys, from Bastar in Madhya Pradesh, wear cowrie-shell ornaments all over their bodies to ward off the evil eye. Other amulets are used in India to help with love, marriage and business.

Bangles are also very popular in India – some women wear so many bangles that they cover their entire arm. Originally, bangles were made of ivory, but nowadays, because ivory is so expensive, plastic ones are used instead. Every major town in India has a special bangle bazaar, where women go to choose the colours of their bangles. The person who sells the bangles always puts them on the woman who buys them. Some bangles are so small that the woman clenches her fist and winces in pain as the bangles are pushed over her hands.

In places such as Iran and Pakistan, women wear heavy and elaborate silver jewellery. Türkmen women, from northeast Iran, Türkmenistan and northern Afghanistan, are given their jewellery by their family and this indicates their wealth and status in the community. Jewellery is worn around the head, arms and shoulders, and some of the most ornate pieces are part of head-dresses and hairstyles.

In northern Thailand and Myanmar (Burma), young Lisu women wear silver jewellery to attract men for marriage. In the villages in the evening, girls pound rice for the next day's meal, and boys may approach and talk to them. Couples exchange silver bracelets as tokens of love. The young people also organize working parties in the fields, where they wear their finest jewellery and sing songs together.

The New Year's festival is the most important ceremony in Lisu society, when all the silver jewellery is worn. The festival celebrates the turning from the old to the new, and all the silver is cleaned. On New Year's Day the women spend a long time dressing themselves in their finest silver, and they come out in the afternoon to dance and sing around the priest's tree.

Make an evil eye charm

You will need:
shells
paints
paintbrush
glue
string

1. Choose a shell that is an oval shape and paint it to look like an eye. Ask an adult to make two small holes in the shell, one at either end.

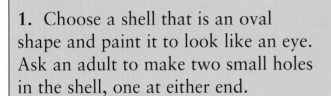

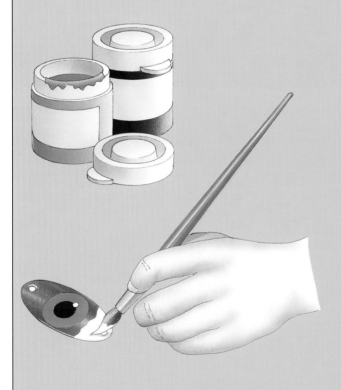

2. Measure and cut a piece of string that is long enough to go over your head and around your neck. Remember to leave enough string to tie a knot at the back.

3. Thread the string through the holes and tie the ends together. You now have an evil eye pendant to protect you and to ward off bad luck. Such pendants are often worn in India and in many other countries.

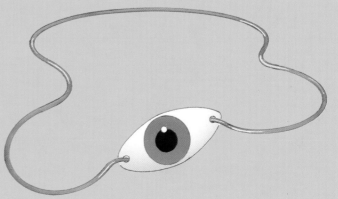

In Indonesia, gold jewellery is worn nowadays by bridal couples. In the past, gold ornaments such as bracelets, anklets and forehead ornaments were owned by the royal families, and were worn at funerals by slaves. The slaves danced so much that they went into a trance and communicated with dead ancestors. This gold jewellery was said to be so powerful that if it was worn by warriors it would protect them from attack.

Not all Indonesian jewellery is made from luxurious items. Thin branches of leathery sea coral called akar bahar are twisted into decorative bracelets and are said to have healing properties. In the Philippines, jewellery is also thought to cure people from sickness. When someone is ill, women perform a 'curing' ceremony, where they go into a trance and wear many strings of beads. In the Andaman Islands, off the coast of India, if a person is suffering from toothache, a necklace made of human bones is wrapped around his or her face as a cure.

Amongst the Naga people who live on the border of India and Myanmar, jewellery is associated with power and prestige. Naga men wear a white and black hornbill feather in dance ceremonies, to show off their military achievements. One hornbill feather indicates that a man has been successful in warfare; two or more feathers mean that he is a great warrior.

The finest jewellery and ornaments are always worn at important ceremonies, such as the spring and harvest festivals. In these ceremonies, the Naga wear all their best ornaments to show that they are strong, healthy warriors. The festivals are lively events that go on for several days, with dances, feasting, drinking and sacrifices. The men stand in a row, holding hands and dancing with their white shell skirts, brightly coloured feather head-dresses and ivory bracelets.

Most Naga jewellery is made from natural materials – shells, feathers, claws, hair, tusks and teeth. The Naga like to dye goats' hair bright red and attach this to their ornaments so that they look lively and colourful. The men used to wear large tusks as jewellery and carry long spears. The women wear necklaces and bracelets made from multi-coloured glass beads.

▲ *Beads are very important to the peoples of the Philippines. They are used in rituals, given as special gifts and treasured as family heirlooms. These women's necklaces represent their wealth.*

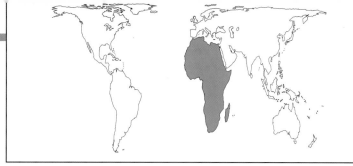

Africa

Nowadays, almost all African peoples wear some form of jewellery, varying from beaded necklaces and ear plugs to elaborately carved ivory and gold ornaments. The jewellery of Africa is a lively and ancient tradition. An oval bone pendant, found in Tunisia, in north Africa, is thought to be about 15,000 years old. Amongst the earliest types of jewellery are beads made of ostrich-egg shells. The San women of the Kalahari desert still thread ostrich-egg shells into headbands and necklaces today.

In north Africa, people prefer to wear silver jewellery, which is considered purer than gold. Silver is said to have healing properties when combined with other precious stones. Topaz is believed to protect against jaundice, emeralds can help fight snake bites, and rubies are thought to be good for the heart.

In the cultures of the Sahara desert, splendid coral, brass and ivory jewellery has been used for centuries in the kingdom of Benin, now in modern Nigeria, and gold ornamentation is popular amongst the Asante of Ghana. Benin still maintains its traditional culture. The king is called the Oba, and only he can wear a complete outfit of coral beads. His chiefs can wear necklaces, bracelets and anklets made of this precious stone, but these must always be returned to the king at their death. Coral is believed to have magical and healing properties.

According to legend, one of the ancient kings of Benin took coral beads from the underwater palace of the sea god, Olokun. It is believed that when the Oba wears his coral costume, he becomes a god himself.

▲ The Oba Akenuza II of Benin in full ceremonial costume. This coral jewellery has been handed down through generations of Obas. Some pieces may be 400 years old.

The Oba and his courtiers also have fine objects made of brass. Herbs and medicines are wiped on to brass bracelets to strengthen and protect the wearer. One brass ornament is hung down from a chief's back, and is called a scorpion. The shiny surface and reddish colour of brass are thought to be both beautiful and threatening enough for the king and his chiefs to wear.

Ivory is also associated with royalty in the kingdom of Benin. Elaborately carved ivory bracelets are worn in special ceremonies in which the king dances. These bracelets keep his coral beads from getting tangled.

The most spectacular gold jewellery in all Africa is worn by the kings and chiefs of the Asante kingdom. Vast amounts of gold adorn the king and his officials. On public occasions, such as the annual Yam Festival, the king wears so much gold on his arms, wrists and fingers that he has to rest his hands on the heads of two small boys who stand in front of him. Traditionally, slaves were forbidden to wear any jewellery, but the higher a person was in society, the more gold jewellery he or she could wear.

Recently it has become fashionable in West Africa to wear gold spectacles. They do not have a lens, but instead have gold wire across them. These glasses stop the wearer from seeing easily, but they are regarded as valuable accessories.

Other metal jewellery is associated with high status. Amongst the Igbo of Nigeria, women wear brass circles the size of plates around their ankles. These are very heavy and make walking difficult. Because these objects are symbols of high rank, women who do not wear the anklets walk as if they are wearing them, to suggest that they are also of high status.

African women are well known for wearing brightly coloured bead jewellery, and this is especially popular among the Masai in Kenya and the Zulu in South Africa. There are at least forty words in the Masai language for different types of beaded decoration. The women wear their jewellery all the time, and because they are nomadic their jewellery is seen as movable wealth. Tens of thousands of tiny glass beads may be strung or sewn to make elaborate, multicoloured ornaments. A woman is not considered beautiful without many layers of colourful beaded necklaces around her neck.

Masai men also wear jewellery. The warriors wear armbands and

▲ *This stiff, flat, beaded collar is worn by a Masai woman in Kenya, to show that she is of marriageable age.*

◀ *This is the foot of Nana Owusu Sampa III, an Asante king from Ghana. He is wearing a gold anklet.*

legbands, which are made by women as a sign of love. Once the men have married they wear much less jewellery, as they have no need to attract women. But the old men always wear snuff containers around their necks, which are given to them by their eldest daughter.

Many different objects are used to create jewellery in Africa. This Uyiyi dancer from Tanzania has strung a light bulb around her neck to make a necklace.

Amongst the Zulu, beadwork is sometimes called a 'language' because it is so complex and precise. Young girls sit in groups and sew beadwork love poems which they give to chosen boys. The colours and designs contain messages, and they can be read as special codes. The different stages of life are marked by different beads. When a girl falls in love, she makes a necklace of a single string of coloured beads. She gives this to her lover and makes a matching set of wrist, ankle and waist beads for herself. If you meet a group of young Zulus, you can tell who is in love with whom by the colours of the beads they wear.

Although traditional jewellery is still being made in Africa, new materials sometimes take the place of the old ones. In South Africa, discarded objects such as Vaseline tin lids are used as pendants. Metal from cars is melted down and used for rings and beads. The Masai have been known to wear ear plugs from a variety of new materials, including rolled-up newspapers, plastic, bottles and buttons.

You will need:
a packet of pasta tubes
string
scissors
many different-coloured
  paints
paintbrush

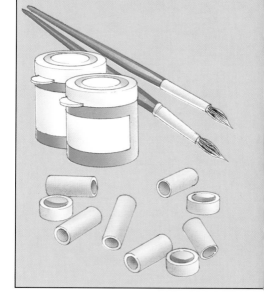

38

Make anklets, bracelets and necklaces

1. Paint the pasta tubes many different colours.

2. Measure how much string is needed to make anklets, bracelets and necklaces to fit you, and cut these lengths. Remember to always leave enough string to tie a knot at the back, and make sure the string for the necklace is quite loose so that you can take it easily on and off.

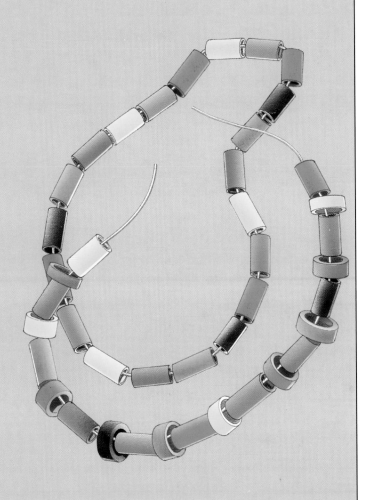

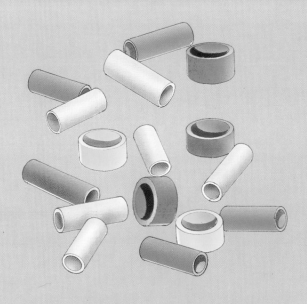

3. Thread the painted pasta tubes on to the different lengths of string and tie a knot at the end. You can then put as many layers as you like around your neck, arms and ankles.

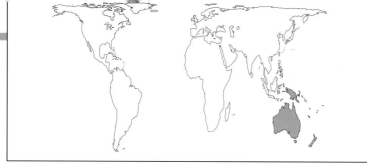

The Pacific

Many different types of jewellery and ornamentation are worn by the peoples of the Pacific region. For centuries, valuable goods have been traded from one island to the next, and sometimes jewellery is exchanged like money. In the Solomon Islands, shell belts are used to buy pigs and canoes. The more shell belts a person owns, the higher his or her status. On special ceremonial occasions the belts are worn for everyone to see.

Shell is used in much of the jewellery and ornamentation of the Solomon Islands. Head ornaments called kap-kap are made of a cream-coloured giant clam shell disc. Delicate, dark brown tortoise-shell designs are fixed on to the clam shell and the kap-kap is then attached to the forehead with a headband made of fibre.

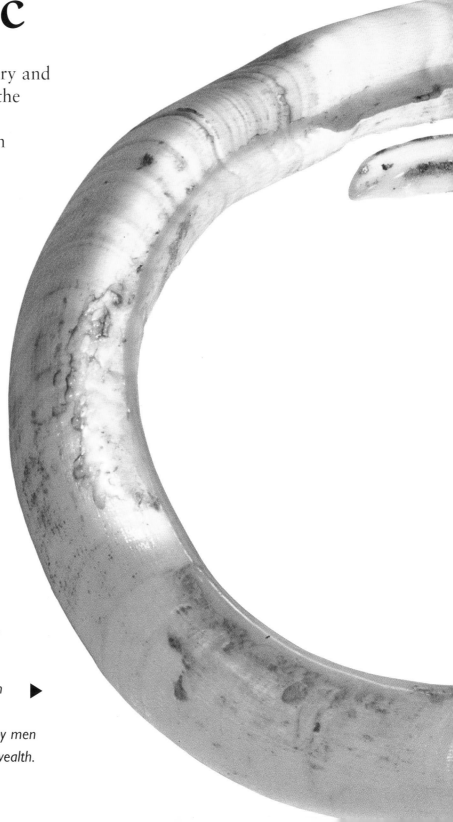

Armbands such as this one from Papua New Guinea are made from pigs' tusks, and are worn by men as decoration and as a sign of wealth. ▶

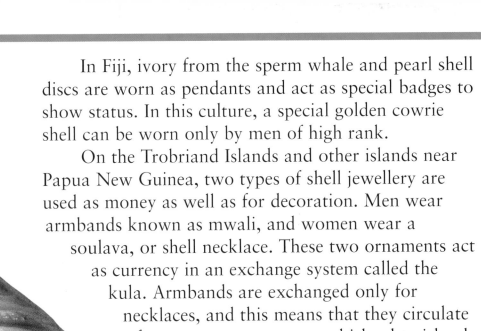

In Fiji, ivory from the sperm whale and pearl shell discs are worn as pendants and act as special badges to show status. In this culture, a special golden cowrie shell can be worn only by men of high rank.

On the Trobriand Islands and other islands near Papua New Guinea, two types of shell jewellery are used as money as well as for decoration. Men wear armbands known as mwali, and women wear a soulava, or shell necklace. These two ornaments act as currency in an exchange system called the kula. Armbands are exchanged only for necklaces, and this means that they circulate from person to person and island to island in an anti-clockwise direction. The necklaces circulate in the opposite direction. The mwali and soulava are worn temporarily to show status. Some pieces of jewellery have become famous. They have names and myths which describe where they have travelled to.

It is not only shell ornaments that are worn to show status in Pacific cultures. Traditionally, brightly coloured feathers were traded between islands and they, too, have become highly valued. In New Zealand, high-ranking Maoris stuck feathers in their hair, and secured them with wooden combs. Some of these feathers were from birds that are now extinct. They were considered so rare that special wooden boxes were carved to store them in, and they were passed on from generation to generation.

Elaborately carved Maori jade breast ornaments called hei-tiki were also passed on as heirlooms. Sometimes the hei-tiki were buried with the owner and then dug up again and worn by the grandchild. These ornaments were more frequently worn by women than men, and the wife of a captured chief always had to send her hei-tiki to the wife of his captor.

The most elaborate and competitive display of ornamentation exists amongst the highland peoples of Papua New Guinea. One of the groups is the Wahgi, who live in the foothills on either side of a valley. For a few months every year, all the different clans come together for a Pig Feast. This ceremony is very competitive. The clans perform in front of crowds of spectators and show off their decorations. If a warrior clan is not very beautifully adorned, it is believed that it may lose its next battle. The men hope that their decoration will be good enough to attract women. They wear long, black bird plumes called Stephanie Tails on their heads, and the dancers help each other to prepare themselves before the dance. Jingling pearl shells are hung from the men's belts. Armbands and other jewellery are added.

Nowadays the Wahgi use many modern objects for jewellery. Some women wear tin lids instead of shells as forehead ornaments, and beer bottle tops

▲ *This hei tiki was made in the eighteenth century and given as a gift to a missionary. Amongst the Maori, hei tikis were said to have special powers.*

are used as earrings. Only the older men now wear elaborate shell ornaments, while younger men push cash notes through their armbands to decorate them. Pink bubble-gum wrappers and red sardine tin labels are sometimes added to the headbands and wigs.

The Australian Aborigines have also adapted their traditional decorations. Small pieces of oval pearl shells were used in some places as forehead ornaments, but nowadays tin lids can be used instead.

The men and women of Melville Island, off the northern coast of Australia, sometimes wear rows of bangles woven from human hair and decorated with seeds or feathers. These are worn as a sign of mourning, particularly for an important or well-liked person.

◀ *Feathers are seen as very valuable by many Pacific peoples. This dancer from Port Moresby, Papua New Guinea, wears brightly coloured feathers as well as shells, grasses and bead decorations.*

In central Australia, pearl shell ornaments called Lonka Lonka are used as charms to attract women. The man sings to the shell, asking lightning to enter it. Later, he ties the shell to his waistband and dances with it on. The woman he wishes to attract will see the lightning flashing on the Lonka Lonka, and be attracted to the man.

The use of human and animal remains is widespread in the jewellery of the Pacific. Human hair is used to attach pearl shell discs in the Marquesas islands. In Samoa, a head-dress known as a tuinga was worn by noble families on festive occasions, and by chiefs in times of war.

This was made of bleached human hair on barkcloth, decorated with feathers, and with a band of shells on the forehead.

In Tahiti and other islands, sharks' teeth and dogs' hair were included in decorative breast ornaments. The male dancers in Hawaii wore boar-tusk bracelets and bands of fibre with dogs' teeth on their legs. Sometimes as many as 1,000 such teeth were used.

But perhaps the most unusual form of decoration was used by the Maori of Taronki. They would thrust the beaks of live birds into holes in their earlobes and wear them as ornaments. You could call this living jewellery!

In Papua New Guinea, men ▶ *wear jewellery and decoration to show their status and power. Feathers, shells, beads and grasses may be used to create the decoration.*

Make a necklace from recycled materials

You will need:
string
sweet wrappers
tin foil
4 toilet roll tubes
a newspaper
glue
different-coloured paints
paintbrush

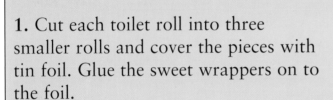

1. Cut each toilet roll into three smaller rolls and cover the pieces with tin foil. Glue the sweet wrappers on to the foil.

2. Measure how much string is needed to create a necklace. Remember to leave plenty of string for tying a knot, and to make the necklace loose enough for taking it on and off.

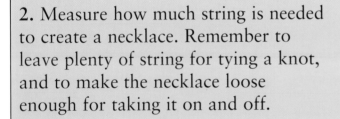

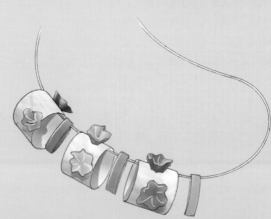

3. Thread the string through the tubes and tie the ends in a knot.

4. Cut thin strips of newspaper. Paint them different colours and leave them to dry. Wrap the strips around the string between the toilet roll sections. Glue their ends together to make hanging loops.

You can use many other types of recycled materials to decorate your necklace, such as egg boxes, yoghurt pot lids and monkey-nut shells.

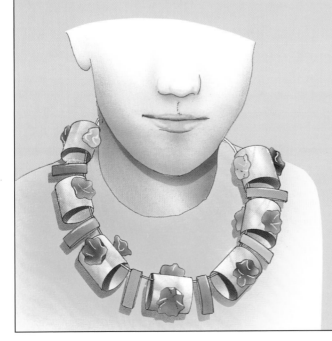

Glossary

Amulet – An object used to protect a person or to ward off evil spirits.

Anglo-Saxons – People from Germany who settled in Britain in the fifth century AD.

Anklet – An ornament that is worn around the ankle.

Barkcloth – A type of cloth made from the bark of a tree.

Bazaar – A market or street of small stalls found in the Middle East and Asia.

Bronze Age – A period in Europe between 2000 and 500 BC, when weapons and tools were first made from bronze.

Clan – A group of families with a common ancestor or surname.

Coronation – A special ceremony for crowning a king or queen.

Courtiers – Attendants at court.

Cowrie – A white shell found in Africa, Asia and the Pacific, used for decoration and as money.

Crest – The symbol of a family or clan.

Epidemic – A disease which affects many people in a community or area.

Evil eye – A look or glance believed to cause great harm, especially to young children or babies.

Guild – A club or organization which is set up to help craftspeople.

Heirlooms – Any objects that have been in a family for generations.

Hindu – A follower of the Indian religion of Hinduism.

Hornbill – A bird from Africa and Asia that has a very large beak.

Inlaid – Objects or jewels set in the surface of a piece of jewellery or furniture.

Inscription – A signature or sentence carved or engraved on to a coin or piece of jewellery.

Iron Age – The period following the Bronze Age in Europe, in which there was an increase in people making iron tools and weapons.

Jade – A semiprecious stone which can vary in colour from white to green. It is often used in making ornaments and jewellery.

Macaw – A large tropical parrot from South America, which has a long tail and brightly coloured feathers.

Migrate – To move from one place or country and settle in another.

Mourning – Feelings or actions which show a person's sadness after the death of someone.

Muslim – A follower of the religion of Islam.

Mythology – A group of myths associated with a particular culture.

Nomadic – A word which describes people who move from place to place to find land for their animals and to grow food.

Oba – The name of the kings of Benin, West Africa.

Ocelot – A jaguar-like animal with a dark-spotted brown coat, which lives in Central and South America.

Plumage – Layers of feathers covering a bird's body.

Plundered – Stolen.

Prestige – A person's status or rank in society.

Rank – A person's official position within a society or organization.

Re-cast – To melt a metal object down and reshape it into something else.

Rosehip – The berry-like fruit of a rose plant.

Snuff – Finely powdered tobacco for sniffing up the nose.

Status – A person's position within a society or organization.

Surrealist – Unreal or dream-like.

Synthetic – Made from artifical or unnatural materials.

Talisman – An object which has magical or protective powers.

Trance – A strange feeling, like being in a dream.

Vikings – Danish, Norwegian and Swedish people who lived in Europe in the eighth to eleventh centuries AD.

Books to Read

Fun with African Beads: A Book and Kit by Liz Bigham and Janet Coles (British Museum Press, 1999)

Kids Around the World Create: The Best Crafts and Activities from Many Lands by Arlette N. Braman (John Wiley & Sons Inc., 1999)

Making Jewellery (Step-by-step) by Sara Grisewood and Jim Robins (Kingfisher, 1999)

People Around the World by Anthony Mason (Kingfisher, 2002)

Peoples of the World (Internet-linked) by A. Claybourne and G. Doherty (Usborne, 2001)

Index

The jewellery and accessories in this book come from many different peoples. Various types of jewellery and accessories are listed in the index, such as 'necklaces', 'anklets' and 'rings'. If you want to see how jewellery and accessories are used, look at entries such as 'ceremonies' and 'festivals'. You can use the 'peoples' entry to look up jewellery and accessories from the cultures mentioned in this book.